Creepy Crawlies

Pauline Cartwright

Contents

Creepy Crawlies

Creepy crawlies are small.
They like to hide.
They **creep** around the house.
They **crawl** around the garden.
Some of them even crawl on you!

In Your Garden

There are lots of creepy crawlies in your garden!
Look in a flowerbed.
You might see a beetle.

Beetles have two lots of wings.
The top wings are hard, like a shell.

The hard wings open up and the beetle can fly!

Creepy Fact

The Hercules beetle is the longest beetle in the world. Its horns are half as long as its body!

Lots of Legs

Look under a rock.

You might find a centipede or a millipede.

Centipedes and millipedes have long bodies and lots of legs.

Centipedes and millipedes look the same, but they are different.

centipede

Centipedes eat insects and other creepy crawlies. They have claws on their head.

millipede

Millipedes eat rotten leaves and plants.

Creepy Fact

Centipedes have up to 382 legs. Millipedes have up to 750 legs.

Slimy!

Look at the garden path.

You might see a shiny trail.

It looks pretty, but it is a trail of **slime**!

Snails and slugs have no legs.
They glide along on slime.
The slime protects their bodies.
It helps them climb up walls and trees.

snail

slug

Snails and slugs can move along upside-down!

Creepy Fact

Slugs have thousands and thousands of teeth.

In Your House

There are lots of creepy crawlies inside your house!

Spiders

Look up at the walls and roof. You might see a spider!

Spiders spin webs from silk.
They sit on their webs.
They wait for bugs to creep,
crawl and fly into the webs.

Creepy Fact

Spiders wrap bugs in silk, and then drink their blood!

On You!

You may not see them, but there are lots of creepy crawlies on you and your pets!

Fleas

Fleas are tiny insects that live on our pets. Fleas bite the animal that they live on and drink their blood.

Creepy Fact

Fleas can jump really high. They can jump 200 times their own length.

Dust Mites

Dust mites are so small that you can't even see them. Dust mites eat dead skin that falls off you and your pets. Yuck!

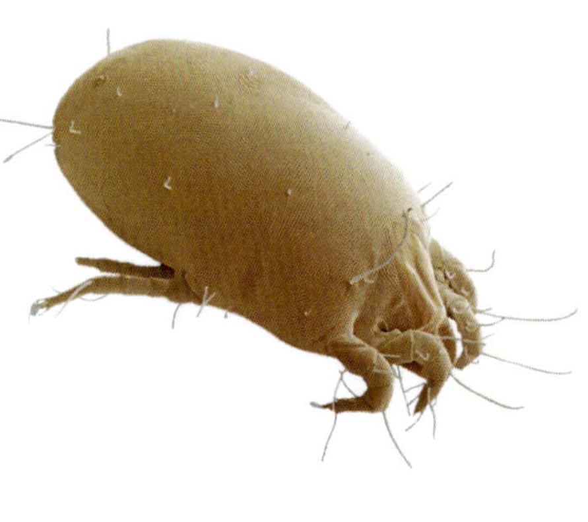

dust mite

Creepy Fact

A dust mite's favourite place to live is... in your bed!

Creepy Fun!

You may not see them, but there are lots of creepy crawlies in the world!

Name the Creepy Crawlies

Which creepy crawly is this?

1

2

3

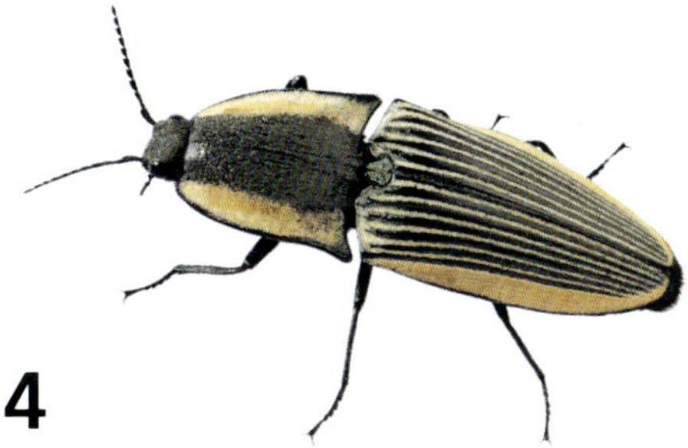

4

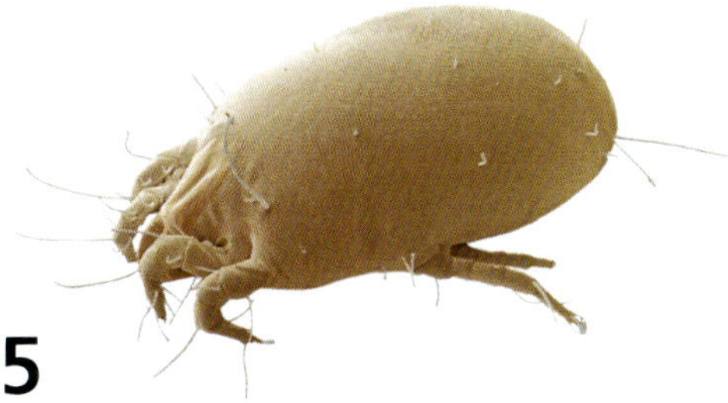

5

1. spider, 2. centipede, 3. millipede, 4. beetle, 5. dust mite

Index